IMAGES
of America

POINT PLEASANT

IMAGES
of America

POINT PLEASANT

Jason Bolte on behalf of the Mason
County Convention and Visitors Bureau

ARCADIA
PUBLISHING

Published by Arcadia Publishing
Charleston, South Carolina

Library of Congress Catalog Card Number: 2006940479

For all general information contact Arcadia Publishing at:
Telephone 843-853-2070
Fax 843-853-0044
E-mail sales@arcadiapublishing.com
For customer service and orders:
Toll-Free 1-888-313-2665

Visit us on the Internet at www.arcadiapublishing.com

To the people of Point Pleasant. This is your story.

CONTENTS

Acknowledgments   6

Introduction   7

1.   Boomtown   9

2.   Rivers Rising   33

3.   River City   55

4.   Postwar Prosperity   75

5.   The Silver Bridge Disaster   93

6.   After the Fall   109

Bibliography   127

Acknowledgments

First and foremost, I would like to thank every person who answered my call for pictures. The response from the community at large was overwhelming, and the process of selecting the images for this book was especially difficult considering the vast collection I assembled. My thanks go out to Molly Yauger, Larry Sayre, Alice Darst, Lois Nibert, Eddie and Mary Sue Kincaid, and the Ball and Spurlock families. My eternal gratitude goes out to Arlona Tait, who displayed the patience of a saint with my erratic and often ill-informed requests. I am indebted to her knowledge and experience with this town. Thanks must also go out to my coworkers, who did not mind when I went missing for days on end to work on this book, and Celesty Fielder, who was kind enough to let me borrow her equipment for weeks on end.

I would also like to thank Jack Fowler, Capt. Charles Henry Stone, and Rod Brand, the resident historians of Point Pleasant. The Point Pleasant River Museum, operated by Jack with the help of the Fout sisters, is a perfect resource for a project such as this, and I am thankful that Jack opened up his photographic coffers for me. Rod Brand, whose volunteer service with the Mason County Convention and Visitors Bureau has no equal, was an equally bountiful reserve for me. He gave me the initial shove for this project, and I have never lost momentum.

Finally, I would like to thank Mike Brown and Karen Fridley. Mike's accidental encounter with my research turned out to be most fortuitous, and his meticulously gathered collections were bounties from the heavens. Karen was another surprising and fortuitous resource. The boxes and boxes of history she has compiled is a fountain of knowledge waiting to be tapped. Thanks again for everyone's help.

INTRODUCTION

Point Pleasant is a town born of crossed paths and star-crossed fortunes. From the mingling waters at *Tu-Endie-Wei*, which means "where the rivers meet" in the Wyandotte tongue, rose a community of outlaws, pioneers, settlers, adventurers, mourners, lovers, and bankers. And just as the rivers flow into one another, meet, and leave again, so does the history of Point Pleasant.

Point Pleasant's first historical mingling occurred on October 10, 1774, when a Virginia militia under Col. Andrew Lewis fought against an army of Shawnee warriors under Chief Cornstalk. The battle took place at the confluence of the Ohio and Kanawha Rivers (Tu-Endie-Wei), and after hours of intense fighting, the Shawnee Nation retreated across the Ohio River. The Virginians had defeated a powerful and organized Native American army, and this battle solidified the Colonial interest in the Ohio Valley. Soon after the battle, Fort Randolph was erected at *Tu-Endie-Wei*, garrisoned with troops to defend the colonists' claims to this hotly contested land. Three years later, Cornstalk was murdered by the Colonists at Fort Randolph, and once again the Virginian men met with the Shawnees, who laid siege to the fort. By the end of the century, the fort was burned and abandoned, but the colonists would begin their settlement of the area.

In 1794, the General Assembly of Virginia granted 200 acres of the Lewis farm (originally owned by Andrew Lewis) to be used to form a community known as Point Pleasant. This name originated from George Washington, who surveyed the land in 1770 as a young man. While Point Pleasant was not officially incorporated until 1833, it still functioned as a thriving river community. Daniel Boone was one of the early settlers in the area. He even represented Mason County when it split from Kanawha County in 1805. By 1835, Point Pleasant contained over 50 buildings, including numerous mills and artisans. The town's population in that year was 240 people, with two resident attorneys and two regular doctors.

The remainder of 19th century progressed slowly for Point Pleasant. It was not until the end of the 19th century and the beginning of the 20th when the little river town become a bustling river city. By the turn of the century, the population had risen to more than 3,000 people, with an established business district. River traffic and railroad traffic brought visitors from all over the nation to Point Pleasant's streets. Wealthy entrepreneurs experimented with new business ventures such as vast shipyards, dry docks, and passenger rail. Before the Revolutionary War, George Washington, seeing the potential of this area, had dreamed of establishing Point Pleasant as the capital city of a new colony, and while he could never bring his idea to fruition, others worked to make that dream a reality.

The town, however, was not always destined to succeed, especially in its early days when it was prone to the whimsies of Mother Nature. It seemed that every time the city gained momentum, a flood swelled beneath its feet, forming a quagmire that was difficult to escape. Just as the town relied upon its rivers to bring people and commerce and progress, the rivers also brought jarring obstacles that were nearly insurmountable. Twice in the town's history the entirety of the region was under water. The 1913 and 1937 floods were rampant examples of natural wrath. The waters mingled, caroused, and retreated like a fool's parade, leaving Point Pleasant reeling and sobered up.

Point Pleasant emerged again as a prosperous city after the Second World War and the erection of flood walls around the city. The Marietta Manufacturing Company, in town since 1915, brought constant and steady jobs at its foundries, shipyards, and factories during the First World War and afterward. The Point Pleasant Ordnance Works, known as the TNT plant, brought industry to the city during the war, laying the foundations for industry for future companies. Point Pleasant remained on the rise, riding the wave of the economic boom to the city. No more floods despoiled the town, river traffic remained steady, and automobile traffic drove ever more people and interest through the town. The nation mingled in Point Pleasant's urban waters as well as in its rivers.

Point Pleasant finally appeared to be in control of its surroundings, and then disaster struck again, shaking the city to its very core. On December 15, 1967, the Silver Bridge, spanning the Ohio River between Point Pleasant and Gallipolis, Ohio, collapsed and fell into the Ohio River. The steel beams and concrete slabs merged with the frigid waters of the Ohio River. When the chaos and destruction was settled and sorted, 46 people died when the bridge fell. Friends, neighbors, and relatives of the entire community had died that night. The town's fiber was trimmed to its core. The loss of the bridge isolated Point Pleasant from the world and the world from Point Pleasant. The city of Daniel Boone and Andrew Lewis was paralyzed, stuck to its point.

With the bridge's collapse came the city's decline. That same year, 1967, the Marietta Manufacturing Company built its final vessel. When the town needed to return to its rivers for economic help, the river could not provide for it. The decades after 1967 were one of intense desperation and waning. The automobile traffic stalled, the riverboats stopped dead in the water, and Point Pleasant was left to its own devices. The post–Silver Bridge era began Point Pleasant's rediscovery of its history, the town gaining a fresh sense of its identity, helping it to prepare for a new age. Museums, such as the West Virginia State Farm Museum, cropped up, odes to Point Pleasant's glorious past. The bicentennial of the Battle of Point Pleasant invigorated the city in 1976, mixing its adventurous past with tenuous present and uncertain future. The last remnant of Point Pleasant's haunting past, the Shadle Bridge, was imploded in 1998. While the bridge fell into the river, it did so by the city's own hand. Since its creation in 1831, Point Pleasant has had its shares of tragedies and inconveniences, but long ago, the city realized that for a successful future, it must reflect and share its past. And so it sits at a final step in its recovery and, more importantly, prepares for a step forward in its future.

One

BOOMTOWN

The definition of a boomtown is a community that tends to rise in status in a relatively short period of time, like a powder keg exploding and sending its soot in many different directions with powerful force. Point Pleasant was such a town. It lay dormant until the 1880s, over 100 years after the Battle of Point Pleasant.

The rise of Point Pleasant began in the latter half of the 19th century, after the Civil War, and leading up through World War II. While important cornerstones of the community slowly emerged, such as the Mason County Court House, railroads, dry docks, and city streets, it was after the Civil War, which the city survived relatively unscathed, when the powder was ignited. From 1833 until 1900, the population of Point Pleasant increased nearly tenfold. By World War II, the population had doubled. This trend is exactly the pattern of the boomtown.

Two important institutions emerged in Point Pleasant in the first half of the 20th century. The first was the rise of a steady banking system, beginning with the Merchants National Bank. The men who nurtured this enterprise also nurtured the community at large, beginning businesses, helping public works, and giving eminence to the blossoming city. The second is the Spencer Hotel, whose colossal stature and central location made it a healthy heart for the growing business district. The rise of the automobile, train stations, and education systems were also key improvements, garnishing the city with opportunity.

The confluence of the Ohio River and the Kanawha River at Point Pleasant is the intersection of the history of America. This junction, called *Tu-Endie-Wei* by the Native Americans, was the location of the Battle of Point Pleasant. The victory at this battle by the Virginian militia ensured the expansion of the American colonies to the Ohio River and eventually past it. Before this

point, the liminal boundary for the colonies was eastward, around the Allegheny Mountains. But because of the victory at this river confluence, named Point Pleasant by George Washington, America could expand into the great western frontier. (Courtesy of Mike Brown.)

OLD LOG HOUSE OF FIRST SETTLEMENT AT POINT PLEASANT W VA GREETINGS

The oldest structure in Point Pleasant, the Mansion House was constructed for use as a tavern. Built in 1796 by Walter Neuman, it has stayed in its original position on the Ohio riverbank near the Kanawha River confluence for over 200 years. The Mansion House was the first hewn-log structure in the county, and for the early part of the 19th century, it served as an inn, church, and general meetinghouse. (Courtesy of Mike Brown.)

Robert Love was born in 1762 in North Carolina. After serving in the Revolutionary War, he married Nancy Rayburn in 1796. Together they settled in 1805 on a 2,700-acre farm outside what would become the town of Point Pleasant, joining Col. Andrew Lewis as one of the first settlers of Mason County. Love died in 1856. Upon his death, the appraisal of his property, including slaves, totaled nearly $10,000. (Courtesy of Karen Fridley.)

Mason County Court House and Cornstalk Monument, Point Pleasant, W. Va.

The Mason County Court House was erected in Point Pleasant in the 1850s and stood at the corner of Sixth and Viand Streets until a new courthouse was erected nearly a century later. In 1899, the remains of Chief Cornstalk, leader of the Shawnee Nation, were buried next to the courthouse, and a small monument was erected to mark his grave. Cornstalk was murdered at Fort Randolph in Point Pleasant in 1777. (Courtesy of Mike Brown.)

Point Pleasant's only involvement in the Civil War was a small skirmish in the spring of 1863. A small detachment of Confederate cavalry marched to Point Pleasant in search of much needed supplies. There they encountered a small regiment of Union troops, who fled to the courthouse for refuge. The Confederates laid siege to the building, firing continuously on the Federals while searching the town. Their search turned up nothing, and they retreated along the Kanawha River. The total casualties for both sides were five dead and seven wounded, including one civilian death. (Courtesy of Mike Brown.)

13

Central Grade School was built in 1890 at a cost of $20,000. It contained eight rooms, a library, and an office. A two-story concrete block adorned the corner lot since 1907, serving the high school students until a larger high school could be built. In a county with as many as 100 one-room school buildings, Central School was a more efficient educational structure. (Courtesy of Rod Brand.)

When the Great War came to an end, American troops returned home to throngs of supporters. This parade in 1919 celebrates the soldiers from Mason County that served in Europe during World War I. Mason County had 28 brave men die in the battlefields of Europe during this war. (Courtesy of Rod Brand.)

This photograph (below), taken on October 7, 1909, depicts Main Street of Point Pleasant three days before the commemoration of the Battle of Point Pleasant. The special issue postcard (right) shows the monument as it stands at Tu-Endie-Wei Park. The monument was unveiled at this celebration. The festival was considered the most important event in Point Pleasant since the battle occurred 132 years prior. Virgil Lewis, the noted historian of West Virginian and a native of Mason County, estimated that 15,000 people attended the ceremony, nearly five times the population of Point Pleasant in 1909. Long processions of noted groups, such as the Masons and the Sons of the American Revolution, marched through the streets alongside descendants of the soldiers who fought in the battle. Ancestors of Andrew and Charles Lewis, the commanders of the Virginia militia at the battle, were also present. (Courtesy of Mike Brown.)

Main Street, looking South, Point Pleasant, W. Va.

During the first part of the 20th century, automobiles emerged as a dominant form of transportation within the city. While Point Pleasant still relied heavily on the rivers, the city's infrastructure evolved to accommodate the emergence of the automobile. Horse-drawn carriages still existed (above), but the entirety of Point Pleasant's business district gave way to the automobile. By 1922, the city had over 3 miles of cement and 2 miles of brick-paved roads. Main Street, especially in the business district, was paved with the latter type of road. To match the growing traffic, there were also 6 miles of cement sidewalks. (Courtesy of Mike Brown.)

Main Street, Looking North from Fourth Street, Point Pleasant, W. Va.

Point Pleasant, in the age before the automobile, was bustling with pedestrians, horse-drawn carriages, and canopies of merchant buildings. Every shop, business, and public building on Main Street offered shade and solace with these overhangs. At times, Main Street resembled an exotic bazaar, an open market with merchants selling handsome wares from open tents. As the 20th century progressed, the canopies disappeared, replaced by street signs or, at the worst, empty buildings. (Courtesy of Mike Brown.)

The heart of Point Pleasant's business district, especially after 1904, was in this block at the intersection of Main and Fourth Streets. The Spencer Hotel, its sister structure the Phoenix Hotel, and J. Freidman and Company were the main accommodations for boat travelers and other visitors. J. Freidman's store was a luxury clothing and shoe store as well as one of the most successful businesses of its time. Numerous businesses operated through the Spencer Hotel's ground level, including the Merchants National Bank, a liquor store, and a barbershop. (Courtesy of Mike Brown.)

The Spencer Hotel was built in 1904 by the Mutual Realty Company of Point Pleasant. It was named in honor of John Samuel Spencer, a noted lawyer and businessman in town. An elegant establishment, the Spencer Hotel was deemed one of the finest hotels in West Virginia, grand enough for any city 10 times the size of Point Pleasant. Its prime location by the Ohio River and its towering structure guaranteed the hotel as the cornerstone of the downtown area. (Courtesy of Mike Brown.)

The executives of Merchants National Bank stand on the steps of the bank after its relocation under the Spencer Hotel. This was one of the most prominent banks in the area, its executives each leading citizens in industry and philanthropy. The bank stayed in this location until 1928. The executives are, from left to right, (first row) Howard Robey and W. W. Riley Sr.; (second row) Alex McCulloch and Taliaferro Stribling Jr. (Courtesy of Rod Brand.)

"Captain" Charles Clendenin Bowyer was president of Merchant's National Bank in the 1920s. He started his career at the bank as a teller and worked his way through the ranks. Bowyer was an avid enthusiast of riverboats, amassing a vast collection of steamboat photographs. He was commonly referred to as "Captain" Bowyer and heavily invested himself in improvements to the rivers around Point Pleasant. (Courtesy of Rod Brand.)

Taliaferro Stribling Jr. followed in his father's footsteps in the banking industry. A lifelong banker, he joined the bank as a teller in 1888. Through his tenure at the bank, one of the major contributing businesses to Point Pleasant, he worked his way up the ranks, eventually earning the position of assistant cashier, a prominent position at that time. Stribling became vice president of the Merchants National Bank in 1921. (Courtesy of Rod Brand.)

Main Street was not the only road to benefit from the rise of the automobile. Running parallel to Main Street, Viand Street also grew in popularity, in part due to the erection of the Shadle Bridge. In the 1920s, major efforts were coordinated to establish highways connecting nearby cities to Point Pleasant, and Viand emerged as a part of this roadway system. By the late 1930s, concrete paving all along Viand aided in the health and effectiveness of this road, as huge paving machines, such as the one in this picture, made Viand Street a safer and more attractive road. (Courtesy of Arlona Tait.)

LUTTON HIGHWAY.

Lutton Highway was a two-lane road running through the outskirts of Point Pleasant. Lined with trees, this scenic highway stretched only seven blocks, but was a beautiful entrance to the city. Initially an uncontracted highway, the Mason County Court House had the highway commissioned for the sake of the county. (Courtesy of Larry P. Sayre.)

20

The Kanawha and Michigan Railroad (K&M) was built primarily for coal traffic, moving coal from the nearby mountains to the states west of the Ohio River. Even after the passenger trains stopped running in Point Pleasant, the coal trains continued to march through town, especially to the nearby power plants that sprung up in the middle of the 20th century. (Courtesy of Mike Brown.)

Union depot, built in 1885, was the main train station for the Kanawha and Michigan Railroad. There were two railroad tracks that ran through town, both intersecting at this depot. The Kanawha and Michigan Railroad ran on a higher track and crossed the Ohio River. The Baltimore and Ohio Railroad crossed at the bottom of the depot and ran east along the Ohio River. The depot was torn down in 1958. (Courtesy of Rod Brand.)

The Kanawha and Michigan Railroad bridge was built in 1918. During its tenure as a passenger track, the Kanawha and Michigan operated a hospital and apartment building for its customers on Sixth Street. During the evening runs, a dining car accompanied the trains, serving sandwiches and refreshments to the passengers. The Kanawha and Michigan also ran through other stops in the county, including Brosia, Beech Hill, Leon, and Arbuckle. Passenger traffic from Point Pleasant to other stops along the Kanawha and Michigan Railroad ended in 1949 and 1950. After the fall of the Silver Bridge, which spanned the river next to the K&M bridge, in 1967, a passenger rail was temporarily established to accommodate the loss of the bridge. (Courtesy of Rod Brand and Mike Brown.)

The large, looming building to the left is Hooff's Opera House. Built in 1900, it was the third opera house in town (the other two burned in 1889 and 1899). Dr. G. W. Hooff designed the building himself. Inside it provided seating for a maximum capacity of 800 people. Occupying the top two stories of the building, the opera house held an elevated stage, two tiers of dressing rooms, rolled drag curtains containing numerous backdrops, and balcony seating affectionately known as "peanut heaven." Touring groups from all over the Ohio Valley came to provide live entertainment. On the ground level were numerous businesses, including the mayor's office, Harper's furniture store, and the Southern Bell Telephone Company. Behind the building were the livery stables, whose entrance was behind the building and whose exit went underneath the building. (Courtesy of Mike Brown.)

Harper's furniture store began operations in 1887. After a fire destroyed the business in the early 1890s, the store moved to another building, functioning until it too was destroyed by fire in 1899. The business reopened with the newly rebuilt Hooff's Opera House, and stayed in business until 1973. George Harper (middle) ran the store after his father died in 1931. (Courtesy of Arlona Tait.)

The Walker IGA (Independent Grocers Association) grocery store was owned and operated by Alonzo Walker (right). Pictured with Kitty Wamsley (left), Walker ran the store for nearly 30 years, starting in 1910 until he began leasing the store to other grocers. Walker also worked at Harper's furniture store, located next to this grocery store. (Courtesy of Arlona Tait.)

Two postal workers play with a postal cart on the steps of the post office. Gordon Jackson (in cart) and Fred Banks (right) used carts such as these prior to the days of parcel post. They would receive mail everyday from six trains at the Kanawha and Michigan Railroad line, and eight trains at the Baltimore and Ohio lines. (Courtesy of the Point Pleasant Post Office.)

The Point Pleasant Post Office opened in 1913. This picture shows its commemoration ceremony during that year. With a total building cost, including up-to-date equipment, of $112,500, it was a state-of-the-art postal building for a city on the rise. Most of the business operated on an elevated first floor, higher up to avoid all but the most devastating floods. Previous to this building, the post office operated out of the first floor of a building on Sixth Street, but it proved to be insufficient space for the amount of postage received daily. After a lengthy public debate over the new location of the post office, the current site was finally agreed upon. For a number of years, a branch of the post office operated in the Heights district in town, but was discontinued in the 1930s. (Courtesy of the Point Pleasant Post Office.)

A group of postal workers pose on the post office steps. The workers are, from left to right, (first row) Griffith T. Smith, Mary Lewis, and Gordon Jackson; (second row) Reba Beale and Donald Beller. Smith was postmaster from 1915 until 1922. (Courtesy of the Point Pleasant Post Office.)

A group of young women stand on the frozen surface of the Kanawha River in the winter of 1936. During the frigid winters, the rivers could become just another part of the icy landscape, a frozen highway rather than a roaring waterway. The women are, from left to right, Mildred Austin, Gladys Peck, Maume Aeiker, and Lida Gibson. (Courtesy of Mitzi Taylor.)

The *Point Pleasant Register* was founded by George Ways Tippett on March 6, 1862. The weekly paper operated out of a small building in the 500 block on Main Street. Tippett was owner, operator, and editor of the paper until his death in 1902, when his son, F. B. Tippett, took over the business. The *Point Pleasant Register* has been in continuous operation as either a weekly or daily newspaper since 1862. In its initial years, the annual subscription rates were $1, always paid in advance. At one time, an advertisement announced that the subscription could be paid with 40 pounds of rags instead of the $1. The *Register* operated in this building until the paper was reorganized in 1930, when it moved to a brick building on the corner of Fifth and Main Streets. (Courtesy of the West Virginia State Farm Museum.)

The *Point Pleasant Register* moved again from its building on Fifth and Main Streets to its current position in 1951, after establishing itself as a daily newspaper. Originally an automobile service station for the Buick company (above), the *Register* moved to this building on Second and Main Streets once it became available. A special feature of this building was its drop box, located on the side of the building, where the newly printed editions of the paper were dropped off during the night. The *Register* remains in this building to this day. (Courtesy of the *Point Pleasant Register*.)

Frank Tippett (below, right) stands with William Balhatchet (below, left) at the Battle of Point Pleasant monument in 1910. Frank Tippett, born in 1870, was the son of George Ways Tippett, and one of his many children who followed in his father's footsteps as a professional printer. His brother, James Bell Tippett, owned and operated a furniture store and undertaking establishment. The Tippetts were a very successful family in the early days of Point Pleasant, owning multiple retail stores, including the Merchant and Tailor store operated by C. C. Tippett (left). (Courtesy of Rod Brand.)

John Brown's Grocery Store, operating in the 500 block of Main Street from the 1920s until the 1960s, was a popular grocery store in the area. It was one of the last grocery stores to allow farmers to trade their farm goods, such as eggs, fresh veggies, etc., for items in the store. These clerks, working in the store in 1928, helped conduct one of the most successful grocery stores in Point Pleasant's history. The owner of the store, John Brown, died in 1974. (Courtesy of Eddie and Mary Sue Kincaid.)

Howard Love (left) and Wayne Kincaid (right) work the meat counter of Evans No. 5 grocery store. Wayne Kincaid served in World War II from October 1942 until December 1945. After one and a half years in Alaska, he arrived in Nagasaki, Japan, two weeks after the atomic bomb was dropped on that city. Before and after the war, Kincaid worked as a grocer and butcher in Point Pleasant. (Courtesy of Eddie and Mary Sue Kincaid.)

In 1930, the West Virginia Bridge Commission authorized a bridge spanning the Kanawha River between Point Pleasant and Henderson, West Virginia. Constructed by the Holmes Constructions Company, it had a length of 1,664 feet. The Shadle Bridge (above) opened to the public on August 12, 1931, and was declared toll free on July 4, 1945. Named after the head of the bridge commission, H. E. Shadle, it helped to usher in the age of the automobile. Before its construction, ferries like the one floating under the bridge (above) carried people, livestock, and automobiles across the river. (Courtesy of the Point Pleasant Post Office and Mike Brown.)

Kanawha River Shadle Bridge, Point Pleasant, W. Va.

Two

RIVERS RISING

The precarious position of Point Pleasant at the confluence of two major rivers, the Ohio River and the Kanawha River, made the city extremely vulnerable to the finicky whims of its natural surroundings. With the growth of the city came its inverse decline when natural disasters struck its burgeoning foundations.

From 1880 until 1948, floods were a major problem for Point Pleasant. While the city did flood before this time, the devastation from those floods was not on the same level as the major and minor ones from this era, as more was at stake and more was generally lost. Some years had multiple floods within a few weeks of each other, making the burden of preparation for unknown disaster even more worrisome. This flooding, while nothing new to the region, was nonetheless prohibitive of positive growth.

The two major floods in 1913 and 1937 were especially dangerous to the welfare of the city. Despite occurring in the fallow winter months, they were nonetheless painful reminders of the insecure position of the town. The 1913 flood did bring some foresight, however, as new buildings were erected with the thought of major flooding in mind. Important structures like the post office carefully considered flooding during construction.

The 1937 flood brought the most change, however, as citizens fed up with nearly 50 years of incurring nature's wrath decided to fight back against it. As civic groups pondered ways to counteract the floods, Point Pleasant was left with a choice: either stay on its current path and ride the storm or move their tents entirely in hopes of avoiding the storm. The plucky citizens of the city chose the former, and the structural integrity of the city weathered the floods for 15 more years, until flood walls granted by the federal government helped to end their troubles.

The Methodist Episcopalian Church was one of the closest churches to the confluence of the Ohio and Kanawha Rivers when these rivers flooded in 1907. In this year, the flood stage was only high enough to cover the steps leading to the entrance of the church. While traveling was difficult, the river was not high enough to halt church services. (Courtesy of Mike Brown.)

There were two floods in the winter of 1907. The first flood, on January 19, crested at 52.2 feet, while the second flood, on March 17, crested at 55.1 feet. Flood stage for the Ohio River begins at 41 feet. The Ohio River had not flooded in five years. This was the worst year of flooding since 1884, when the river reached a height of 60.8 feet. (Courtesy of Mike Brown.)

34

Hooff's Opera House had already dealt with two fires when a flood occurred in 1907. The flood inundated the businesses at the base of the building, but never reached high enough to damage the performance hall of the opera house, which was elevated on the second and third floors of the building. (Courtesy of Mike Brown.)

After the river receded to its normal level, all members of the community were needed to clean up the streets and restore the town. Children were no exception, as a group of them along with other adult workers, pose for a photograph during their work on Main Street. (Courtesy of Rod Brand.)

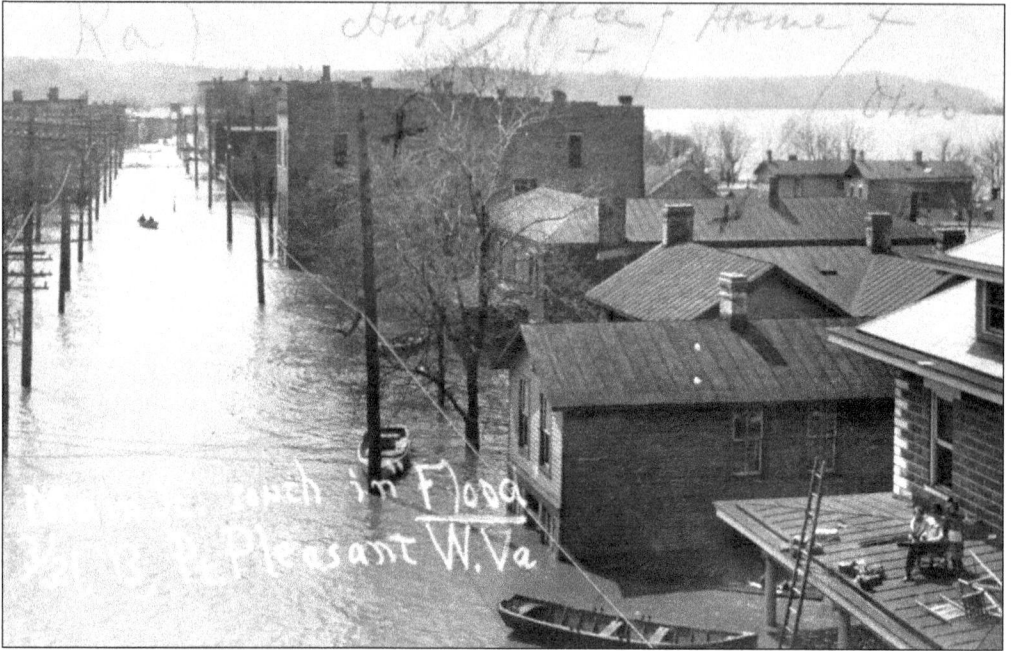

There were two separate floods in 1913. The first occurred in January of that year, but only reached a flood stage of 50.4 feet. The second, cresting on March 30, was more devastating, reaching its historical peak of 62.8 feet. It remained near this level for many days to follow. (Courtesy of Rod Brand.)

Taken from a high hill south of the city, this picture shows the major landmarks of Point Pleasant underwater. In the right foreground are the courthouse and Central School, the latter with its windows lit. To the left are the post office (white building) and the Spencer Hotel. In the background, beyond the river, is Gallipolis, Ohio, with many of the buildings nearly covered in water. (Courtesy of Rod Brand.)

Despite the cold weather and dreary conditions, the citizens of Point Pleasant resumed their daily lives during the floods, conducting business as best they could via rowboat. At this point in the 1913 flood, the water was only high enough to reach the first floor of many buildings, but it would soon reach the second story of many of them. (Courtesy of Rod Brand.)

The Spencer Hotel's sign normally loomed over pedestrians as they walked underneath it, but during the 1913 floods, it was just another obstacle protruding into the waterway for passing rowboats to avoid. It was not uncommon for the flooded streets to have as much traffic as the non-flooded streets, albeit with rowboats instead of automobiles or carriages. (Courtesy of Rod Brand.)

The flood of 1915 was just another midwinter flood when compared to the devastating floodwaters of two years prior. In 1915, the flood stage was a mere 49.8 feet of water, cresting on February 5. By the time this picture was taken, the water had receded to a point where boats were unnecessary yet still ubiquitous on the streets, sitting motionless in empty spaces by the roadside. Pedestrian traffic returned to the city, and it could resume its normal business affairs. By 1915, the flooding river had become a public nuisance to Point Pleasant, as many of its citizens had already experienced numerous floods within a few short years. (Courtesy of Mike Brown.)

As soon as the floodwaters began to rise, the city normally temporarily blocked the sale of alcohol in the taverns and saloons, hoping to avoid accidental "death by drowning" by drunks, as well as "nocturnal rowdyism." It was not universally adhered to, as this boat of people in the 1936 flood enjoy a cold beer as they float down Main Street. (Courtesy of Eddie and Mary Sue Kincaid.)

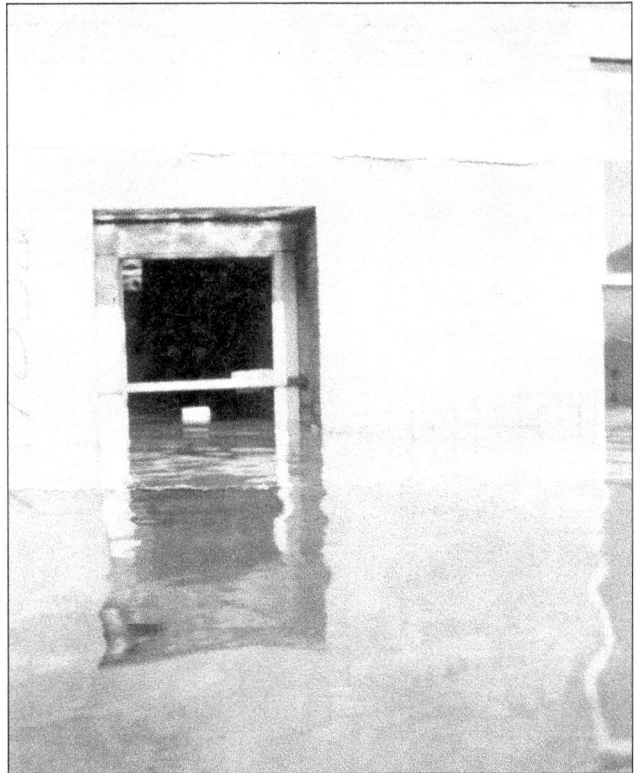

The 1937 flood was another of the historically devastating floods, engulfing the entire Ohio Valley for weeks on end with high water amidst cold temperatures. Watching the floodwaters rise was an anxious experience. This close-up picture of a building's first-story doorway attests to this anxiety, as the doorway would be completely covered only a few days later. (Courtesy of Arlona Tait.)

The typical procedure during floods was to move all the furniture from the first floor of a building to the second floor, if a building had a second floor. From that point, it was a waiting game, as people were generally stuck inside of their buildings unless they owned a rowboat. This particular family was given the luxury of a balcony. During the worst flood years, this balcony would be more like a porch, the floodwaters reaching high enough to graze the bottom of it. (Courtesy of Arlona Tait.)

Tu-Endie-Wei was most prone to flood damage due to its position at the intersection of the Kanawha and Ohio Rivers. The 1937 flood was particularly devastating to the Mansion House (left). The building stood in that position for nearly 150 years, and the fact that it survived each of the previous floods is remarkable for such an ancient structure. (Courtesy of Rod Brand.)

Even the Marietta Manufacturing Company received some flooding during the 1937 flood. Two days after the river reached its highest point, January 29, 1937, the river had only dropped a few inches. The boat in the background of the picture was launched a few days before the floodwaters rose and floated back to the Marietta Manufacturing plant while the waters were high. (Courtesy of the Point Pleasant River Museum.)

Many homes were overturned during the floods, supported by weak foundations and flimsy construction. The average home was only one story tall, the roof barely peeking out above the water. Those that had more than one story spent days before and after the flood hauling furniture to the upper floors with no guarantee that the water would not reach that high. (Courtesy of Rod Brand.)

The Point Pleasant area during the 1937 flood, seen here from two separate aerial views, was difficult to distinguish as the rivers inundated the land from the riverbanks to the Appalachian foothills. Henderson, West Virginia, across the Kanawha River, and Gallipolis, Ohio, across the Ohio River, fared an equal amount of flooding, as did most of the Ohio Valley from Pittsburgh through Cincinnati. Much of the flood's damage can be attributed to a lack of preparation, as most estimates forecasted at the worst only a minor flood in the early weeks of 1937. However, this turned out to be a historically devastating flood for the area. (Courtesy of the Point Pleasant River Museum.)

This aerial photograph shows Point Pleasant one day (January 26, 1937) before the flood stage reached its highest historical peak of 62.8 feet. Within 24 hours of this picture, many of the houses at even the highest elevation in town, such as the ones at the bottom of the photograph, would be filled with multiple feet of water. The Heights region of Point Pleasant, so called because of its higher elevation when compared to the downtown area, received major flooding for only the second time in its recent history. While not a heavily populated area of town, it was particularly devastating to some of the businesses that operated from this region, such as the Marietta Manufacturing Company. (Courtesy of the Point Pleasant River Museum.)

Churches were no exception to the ravages of natural disasters. The 1937 flood was the closest Point Pleasant ever came to a biblical flood, washing everything in town with cold water, driving rains, and a rising river. The Southern Methodist Church (above), while spared much of the flood's wrath in previous incarnations, did not go unscathed in the 1937 flood. Much like the Mansion House, which stood a block away, this church was filled through its chapel with the floodwater. The Main Street Baptist Church (below) shared a similar experience. Located up Main Street from the Methodist Church and one of the oldest churches in town, this church could not withstand the floodwaters. (Courtesy of the Point Pleasant River Museum.)

Trinity United Methodist Church was located adjacent to both Central School and the Mason County Court House in 1937. It had survived the onslaught of the Civil War relatively unscathed, when it served as a makeshift hospital after the skirmish in Point Pleasant. But it received more damage from the 1937 flood than throughout an entire war. Its bell tower was the only part of the building to escape unharmed. (Courtesy of the Point Pleasant River Museum.)

This area outside of the courthouse was the end limit of the "Get Point Pleasant Out of the River" movement that followed the 1937 flood. The fire marshal declared the courthouse unsafe and unsanitary after the flood, and Judge Lewis H. Miller refused to hold court in the courthouse until the necessary repairs were made or the courthouse was rebuilt on higher ground. The public voted on moving the courthouse in 1937. The motion overwhelmingly failed. (Courtesy of the Point Pleasant Post Office.)

The Alpine Theater, one of the most popular movie theaters in the area, could not stay open during the flood of 1937 despite all efforts to the contrary. As soon as the waters retreated back into the river, the theater reopened its doors again for a public in desperate need of entertainment. Admission for adults at this time was a quarter, while children paid only a dime. (Courtesy of Roger Clark.)

The movement calling for a removal of Point Pleasant from its low ground to the Heights was very prominent in the months following the 1937 flood. Since they could not get the money for a flood wall, the mass movement of the business district was the next best idea. The movement called for every part of Main Street from the Kanawha River to Sixth Street to move a few miles upriver onto higher ground. (Courtesy of the Point Pleasant Post Office.)

The mass movement initiative was predicated that the buildings, such as the ones in this picture, were too prone to the constantly flooding rivers. By 1937, the river had flooded on such a regular basis, every year for some stretches, with only a few consecutive non-flood years, and that it was detrimental to the overall health of the city. Given that businesses not only lost money due to damage inflicted by the floodwaters but also from the multiple days when their shops were closed, the movement to higher ground would protect the city from all but the most devastating floods. The local papers were especially vocal about the benefits of moving the downtown area, with numerous editorials in favor of the move. When the public voted down the initial phase of that movement (the rebuilding of the courthouse), the "Get Point Pleasant Out of the River" group lost its steam. While Point Pleasant decided to stick to its guns, the downtown area continued to flood for another decade and a half. (Courtesy of Rod Brand.)

The post office was built in 1912 and completed in the early part of 1913. When the 1913 flood swept through Point Pleasant, the floodwaters reached up to the bottom of the curtains in the main office of the post office. Luckily no furniture had been installed, and thus the damage to the post office was minimal (above). The building remained relatively unscathed for many of the floods. Like Hooff's Opera House, the post office conducted business out of its second story. Only the most damaging floods were capable of exacting any damage to its interior, despite the building's close proximity to the Ohio River's bank. The 1937 flood was the last time the waters reached into the offices of the post office, seeping into even its seemingly impenetrable walls (below). (Courtesy of Point Pleasant Post Office.)

The 1937 flood committed an estimated $350,000 in damages to property to the area around Point Pleasant, including Henderson and some Ohio communities. Point Pleasant itself suffered at least $100,000 to its buildings. Some of this damage was repaired using government loans, but that only applied to businesses that were damaged by floodwaters (below). Private homes were left to their own devices. After many years of flooding, the heavy toll of constant rebuilding took its toll on homeowners (above). An unintentional effect of the flood was a stunted growth to its neighborhoods, as houses were difficult to build sturdy enough to withstand seemingly incessant floodwaters. (Courtesy of the Point Pleasant River Museum and Rod Brand.)

The Point Pleasant Presbyterian Church, located on the corner of Eighth and Main Streets, was only in this location for 10 years when the 1937 flood swept through town. Resembling the post office in structure, this church was not immune to the floodwaters either. The church recovered quickly after the flood. (Courtesy of Point Pleasant River Museum.)

The schools of Point Pleasant were not particularly efficient in recovering from the periodic flooding. While some businesses managed to open within days of the floodwaters receding, schools like the Central School were closed for nearly a month following the 1937 flood. (Courtesy of the Point Pleasant River Museum.)

The department store G. C. Murphy's, a local establishment, suffered substantial damage to its ground-level storefront in the 1937 and 1948 floods. However, business during this time was not hampered to any great extent, especially considering the increased demand of supplies for residents in the area. In both flood times, the store continued operations through its upper stories, from windows (right), and back doors, allowing those that needed food, clothing, and other necessities access during a natural disaster of such great magnitude. The store opened its doors again a month after the 1937 flood and continued to flourish despite the damage to its interior. (Courtesy of the Point Pleasant Post Office.)

Grocery stores and butcher shops were affected twofold in flood times. Not only were they damaged physically by the floodwater, but their supply from local farmers was also truncated. Throughout the Ohio Valley, farms overwhelmed by the rising rivers received significant damage to soil, food storage facilities, and livestock. (Courtesy of Eddie and Mary Sue Kincaid.)

The last major flood of Point Pleasant occurred in 1948, when the river crested twice, reaching a height of 55.4 feet and 43.7 feet. The State Theater, trying to make the best of the deluge, changed its marquee, punning on a popular movie of the time and bringing some much needed humor to a damp city. *Gone with the Wind* thus became "Gone with the Flood." (Courtesy of the U.S. Department of Agriculture.)

Point Pleasant finally constructed flood walls around the city in 1951, after many years of appeals to the federal government for aid. In 1938, Congress passed the Flood Control Act in response to rampant floods of 1937. It was under this act that the city of Point Pleasant appealed the government. The Army Corps of Engineers began work on the flood walls in 1948. When the project was completed, 7,300 feet of concrete walls, ranging from 3.5 feet to 50 feet in height, surrounded the city of Point Pleasant. Special sections of the flood wall remain open, with concrete inserts to be applied for emergency situations. It is a very rare occasion, however, for these inserts to be installed. While part of the reason for the lack of floods since 1951 can be attributed to the flood walls, another reason is the regulation and control of the Ohio River through its lock and dam system. By the middle of the 20th century, the normally wild Ohio River was tamed by this system, with the river remaining at a relatively constant level throughout the year. (Courtesy of the City of Point Pleasant.)

While no major flood has occurred in Point Pleasant for nearly 50 years, it has not stopped the town from flooding in certain capacities. This picture is of Krodel Park in 1997. Located a mile east of downtown and near the Kanawha River bank, this park rests in an especially low-lying area of town. During heavy rains, parts of town such as this are prone to flooding, even despite the flood walls. However, the waters are not particularly devastating, as much of this comes from groundwater swells and nearby creeks as opposed to the big rivers next to the city. (Courtesy of the City of Point Pleasant.)

Three

RIVER CITY

The evolution of Point Pleasant as a river city is a natural one. Not only does it sit neatly as a halfway point between two major cities on the Ohio River (Cincinnati and Pittsburgh), but it is also a gateway to the Kanawha River, where industrial materials such as coal continue to pour out. Point Pleasant became the epitome of a river town, controlling and patrolling the crossroads of its intersection with the zeal and ready ambition of an eager toll keeper.

The city was a popular destination for all types of river craft, from passenger steamboats transporting people upriver to Pittsburgh, to floating hotels, showboats, and other pleasure craft. The Kanawha and Ohio riverbanks were usually filled with boats, some docking overnight to rest, its passengers staying in town, to others being serviced at the harbor and dock companies. Small boat building enterprises were a part of the riverboat industry, but the majority of these worked as repair sites for a steady stream of riverboats.

Point Pleasant truly became a river city in 1917 when the Marietta Manufacturing Company opened its doors inside the city limits. Not only did this company provide a massive expanse of employment opportunities and hard work endeavors common to the city, but it established the town as an epicenter of solid craftsmanship of river craft. Boats were always produced at Point Pleasant, but never at the scale, efficiency, and level of expertise required at Marietta Manufacturing. The company brought a thoroughbred identity to Point Pleasant, enhancing the one that already existed. This chapter shows how it so happened, starting with its pedigree and then showing where the pedigree came from.

This building held the main offices of the Marietta Manufacturing Company on North Main Street. The company was incorporated in Point Pleasant in 1915, and moved all operations to the city by 1917. The boats built by this company were used throughout all of the major American waterway systems, as well as oceangoing craft throughout the world. (Courtesy of Mike Brown.)

An aerial view of the Marietta Manufacturing Company's facilities depicts the vast expanse of land necessary for this company. The launching area along the banks of the Ohio River was often busy with ships needing repairs, ships being built, or ships requiring general servicing. (Courtesy of the Point Pleasant River Museum.)

The advertising motto of the Marietta Manufacturing Company was "Made Mechanically Correct." Due to the skill of its workers and the professional quality it produced in its shipyards, the word Marietta was known throughout the Mississippi river system as a mark of quality. (Courtesy of Mike Brown.)

The Marietta Manufacturing Company began as a stove manufacturing company and had no intentions of being a shipbuilding company. However, due to the demand of ships and its prime location in Point Pleasant, the evolution to a full-scale shipyard was inevitable. Within a decade of its incorporation in Point Pleasant, the company was among the top ship construction companies in the nation. (Courtesy of Mike Brown.)

Throughout its 60-year history in Point Pleasant, the Marietta Manufacturing Company produced gigantic, hulking ships for both river systems and ocean voyages. As one of the main employers in Point Pleasant, the entire town became involved in the river industry. The popularity of the company ensured jobs for the town, keeping workers busy constructing numerous ships at a time. (Courtesy of Mike Brown.)

This airplane, while toting the name of the Marietta Manufacturing Company, was not built by the shipyard. Even though the company was a master at producing enormous machines, this plane was used primarily for advertising and other displays of public spectacle on behalf of the company. (Courtesy of Eddie and Mary Sue Kincaid.)

LAUNCHING A BOAT, MARIETTA MFG. CO.

Boat launches from the Marietta Manufacturing Company were incredible sights to behold. Crowds would usually watch as the newly built ships would slide into the water sideways, tilting so far that they nearly capsized, before righting themselves. The entire process took less than a minute. (Courtesy of Larry Sayre.)

In the 1920s, a group of executives of the Marietta Manufacturing Company pose for a photograph during a launching event. They are, from left to right, Mr. and Mrs. C. O. Weissenburger, Charlotte Weissenburger, Werner Streuben, and Dennis Park. (Courtesy of the Point Pleasant River Museum.)

59

Charles Weissenburger became president of the Marietta Manufacturing Company in 1929 after the death of Walter Windsor, the man who brought the company to Point Pleasant. Weissenburger's major contribution was to establish the construction of oceangoing vessels at the Marietta Manufacturing Company, previously unheard of for an inland shipyard. (Courtesy of the Point Pleasant River Museum.)

The St. Louis was one of the four all-steel towboats built by the Marietta Manufacturing Company for government agencies. Launched in 1921, it was one of the most powerful of the four steel towboats constructed by the company, with a triple expansion engine capable of about 2,500 horsepower. (Courtesy of Mike Brown.)

Fleet of All Steel Craft being outfitted, Plant of Marietta Manufacturing Co., Point Pleasant, W. Va.

World War I brought an increased demand in government steamers and the Marietta, whose shipyard was relatively new and furnished with up-to-date equipment, was a perfect company for new ship production. Four all-steel steam towboats were under construction by the company for government agencies in 1919, and by 1921, the ships began to roll out. The *Cairo* (below), *St. Louis*, *Memphis*, and *Boston* were unique ships on the American waterways and also among the most powerful. Hailed for its technical merits, the federal government's Inland Waterways Corporation advertised these towboats as "an important part in bringing back national confidence in our Western rivers" (above). (Courtesy of Mike Brown.)

Launching U. S. Government Steamer Cairo, Plant of Marietta Manufacturing Co., Point Pleasant, W. Va.

The *Weber W. Sebald* rests in dry dock at the Marietta Manufacturing Company. While the shipyard was primarily used to build watercraft, it was also a functioning and popular repair dock, especially given its position on the Ohio River as a halfway point between Cincinnati and Pittsburgh. This boat was prominent in the 1950s as a steamer towboat along the Ohio and Kanawha Rivers. In 1956, it raced another steamer towboat, the *J. T. Hatfield*, between Procterville and Huntington. The race was broadcast on national television. The *Weber W. Sebald* sunk in the Kanawha River in 1970. (Courtesy of the Point Pleasant River Museum.)

One of the most unusual stunts performed by the Marietta Manufacturing Company was the week they paid their employees entirely in silver dollars. Every single employee, such as this group of dockworkers (above) or this blacksmith (bottom image, left) and night watchman (bottom image, right), was issued pockets full of silver dollars instead of their normal paycheck. For weeks afterward, every retail business, restaurant, and office was inundated with these coins. Not only did this stunt prove how pervasive the company was for Point Pleasant, it also showcased the good-natured attitude and cunning business sense of its executives. (Courtesy of the Point Pleasant River Museum and Arlona Tait.)

The *J. T. Hatfield* was built in Point Pleasant in 1904. It had a special whistle cast by the J. W. C. Heslop Company of Point Pleasant. A steamer towboat of the Mississippi system, the boat was disabled in 1930. After its dismantling, the roof bell went to the Methodist Church at Lock 11 near Point Pleasant. (Courtesy of Mike Brown.)

The *Island Queen* spent most of its life at Coney Island in Cincinnati. This picture, taken on May 1, 1912, captures the *Island Queen* on one of its special excursions outside of Cincinnati. During one of these excursions for citizens of Gallipolis and Point Pleasant, the boat hit a low-hanging wire, snapping its smokestacks off and injuring some on deck. (Courtesy of Mike Brown.)

In 1913, the A. M. *Scott*, while docked in Point Pleasant, was converted from an oil-burning craft to a coal-burning craft. The boat's design was pioneering for propeller towboats, a boat well ahead of its time. Its particular type of towboat became popular well after it was decommissioned in 1928. (Courtesy of Mike Brown.)

The steamer *Fairmont* is docked in Point Pleasant on July 28, 1917. It was an early steam towboat, used primarily for towing showboats along the Mississippi system. This boat was decommissioned in 1922. (Courtesy of Mike Brown.)

Coal Fleet at Kanawha Dock, Pt. Pleasant, W. Va.

Steamers { Florence Marmet
Andrews
G. W. Thomas

These steamer towboats, docked on the Kanawha River in the early 1900s, were common sights in Point Pleasant. The *Florence Marmet* was built in Point Pleasant, and featured a spectacular gilded eagle on its pilothouse. This statue could be seen from far distances all around. The boat was condemned in 1915 and sunk in ice in 1918. (Courtesy of Mike Brown.)

B. & O. R. R. BRIDGE ACROSS THE KANAWHA AND FLEET OF BOATS.
POINT PLEASANT, W. VA.

The Baltimore and Ohio Railroad bridge was torn down and replaced with a modern bridge in 1947. For nearly 60 years, the bridge stood and operated as a popular passenger train bridge, with as many as six passenger trains passing daily through town. A common sight along the river, this image shows the two dominant forms of travel in Point Pleasant during the first part of the 20th century. (Courtesy of Mike Brown.)

A crowd gathers on the banks of the Kanawha River near Tu-Endie-Wei Park. The mouth of the Kanawha was a busy intersecting point for river traffic, with boats on their way to Charleston passing coal barges from Pittsburgh or steamboats from Cincinnati. (Courtesy of Mike Brown.)

The *Dorothy Adgate*, photographed here at Point Pleasant on August 23, 1914, had a very cursed history. A steam towboat on the Ohio, it ran into a lock in 1914, sinking into the water. After repairs, it lasted until 1919, when it caught fire. Repaired another time, it lasted, without major incident, until 1930. (Courtesy of Mike Brown.)

The *Sophia M. Gardner* was built in Point Pleasant in 1912. It did not last very long on the Ohio system, but instead moved to the Missouri and Mississippi Rivers as a steamer towboat. It sank in a windstorm at the Missouri City Bend on April 3, 1917. (Courtesy of Mike Brown.)

The *Tacoma* was the longest-lasting packet steamboat on the Ohio River, enduring through 39 years. In this picture, it is backing out of the Kanawha River wharf outside of Point Pleasant on December 22, 1914. This boat burned in a fire that consumed many other boats, including the *Island Queen*, outside of Coney Island, Cincinnati. (Courtesy of Mike Brown.)

The *Greenwood*, pictured as it leaves Point Pleasant, was "the goose that laid the golden egg" for the Greene Line Steamboat Company. It passed Point Pleasant often while on its Pittsburgh-Parkersburg-Charleston routes. It was seriously damaged in 1925 when another steamer ship backed into it. (Courtesy of Mike Brown.)

Floating Theatre, Point Pleasant, W. Va.

Showboats were popular along the Ohio River. The famous showboat *Princess* was built in Point Pleasant as part of a citywide effort to aid a theater company falling on hard times. "Captain" C. C. Bowyer found a condemned government dump scow, donating it to the theater group, who had it converted into the floating theater, *Princess*. (Courtesy of Mike Brown.)

The steamer ship *Homer Smith* was a local treasure. Owned and operated by the Security Steamboat Company of Point Pleasant, it was named after Homer Smith, owner of the Spencer Hotel. The ship was advertised as a floating hotel, a perfect companion to Smith's land-based hotels. The picture (below) is of the *Homer Smith*'s maiden voyage on April 11, 1915. Referred to as "the Queen and Pride of Western Waters," it boasted an occupancy capacity of 3,000 people. Among the luxuries available during its voyages were a popcorn roaster, soda fountain, ice cream parlor, orchestra, and choir. This ship burned outside of Pittsburgh in 1931. (Courtesy of Mike Brown.)

The Kanawha Dock was a large operation, employing 40 workers. It began business in Point Pleasant on November 17, 1902, after being purchased from the Excel Docks of B. F. Flesher in Middleport, Ohio. The docks could accommodate ships up to 50 feet by 200 feet in size, and could hold up to two ships at a time. (Courtesy of Mike Brown.)

The Kanawha harbor was a busy port, often receiving and servicing numerous ships each day. In the bottom of the picture, the Kanawha ferry, a flat boat pushed across the river with a long pole, transports passengers across the river in the days before the Shadle Bridge. (Courtesy of Mike Brown.)

LOCK 11, KANAWHA RIVER, POINT PLEASANT, W. VA.

The Kanawha River was the first river in America to have a complete navigation system installed. The locks and dams of the Kanawha, spanning from Kanawha Falls to Point Pleasant, were constructed in the 1880s and 1890s for a price of $3,885,200. Lock 11 (below), at the mouth of the Kanawha by Point Pleasant, was completed in 1897. After the navigation system was complete, the Kanawha River grew in popularity, especially for coal barges. Within 20 years of the lock's construction, coal transportation along the Kanawha nearly tripled. While the locks were erected particularly for riverboats, it was also a pleasant leisure spot (above). (Courtesy of Mike Brown and Larry Sayre.)

46502 LOCK No. 11, BIG KANAWHA RIVER, PT. PLEASANT, W. VA.

The ferryboat *Charles Henry Stone* in the bottom of the picture was the main ferry for crossing the Kanawha River from Point Pleasant to Henderson, West Virginia. Operated by the Stone family, the ship was named for Capt. Charles Henry Stone, who drove the ferry from his childhood until he was a young man. When the Shadle Bridge began construction, the ferry was phased out, finally closing with the bridge's opening in 1931. (Courtesy of Mike Brown.)

The *Ann Bailey* was the main ferry in operation across the Ohio River from Point Pleasant to Gallipolis, Ohio. It lasted on the river from 1901 until 1928. The construction of the Silver Bridge in 1928 made the *Ann Bailey* an outdated mode of river transportation. Her last captain was Captain McDade. While the boat was named for a historical personage, it was egregiously misspelled, as the original "Mad" Anne Bailey retained the silent "e" in her name. Despite the mistake, the ferry was still popular in Point Pleasant. (Courtesy of Mike Brown.)

Four

POSTWAR PROSPERITY

Like much of the nation, the Second World War brought an increased demand for industry, perseverance, and economy to struggling communities. Point Pleasant was no exception. Because of its established prominence among the world's waterways through the Marietta Manufacturing Company, the wave of positive growth and expansion was much easier for Point Pleasant to ride.

The 1940s, 1950s, and 1960s were also a time of establishing the culture of Point Pleasant as well. Due to the increased stability in the town, the citizens could carve out an identity outside of itself, one not completely dominated by rivers or boats. Much like in the early 20th century, Point Pleasant was reintroduced into the world. The growing highway systems allowed travelers to tour the city streets anew. Other industries returned to the city, such as coal-burning power plants, which was another source of steady employment. The locks and dams along the Ohio River prevented severe flooding throughout this period, allowing agriculture in Point Pleasant and Mason County to flourish again. Popular culture arose from television sets and movie theaters. The streets of Point Pleasant bustled during the day with tourists, traffic from its bridges, and customers shopping through the many stores and businesses along Main Street. Nightlife entertainment also flourished, as the beer halls, taverns, and movie theaters were crowded on a regular basis. Point Pleasant became part of the ever-shrinking world in the new global village. This era was a time of peace, of calm, of prosperity and new ideas, and the retention and expansion of old ones.

During World War II, public land outside of Point Pleasant was converted into an expansive ordnance and munitions area. From this encampment, known as the TNT area to locals, explosives and chemicals were produced for the war effort. Begun in 1943, this ordnance area included massive acid storage units (below) as well as numerous construction buildings, barracks, power plants, and factories. The explosives were stored in immense concrete bunkers, dubbed "igloos" by locals. After World War II ended, the ordnance area ceased operations and disbanded, as all the troops evacuated the area, leaving the buildings empty. Many of these buildings are still standing in 2007. (Courtesy of the Point Pleasant River Museum.)

Wayne Kincaid's Meat Mart opened its doors after World War II, staying in business until 1966. Alonzo "Buck" Dickens stands next to the Meat Mart truck, which made special deliveries from the butcher shop to homes and businesses around town. The Meat Mart specialized in baked hams and was on call 24 hours a day to visiting riverboats. (Courtesy of Eddie and Mary Sue Kincaid.)

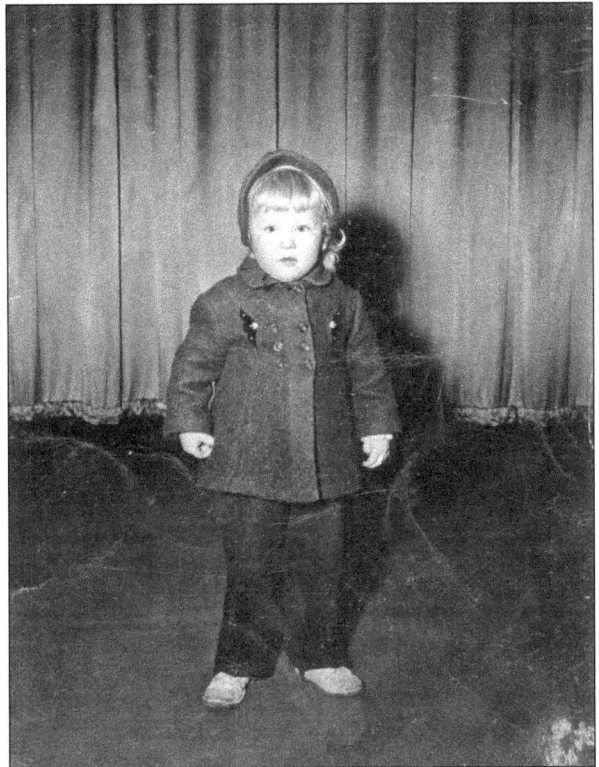

A special ceremony was held on March 7, 1948, at the State Theater. The ceremony was in honor of Dr. Edward McElfresh, a longtime physician in town, who traveled by any means to answer house calls day or night. When the entire town celebrated Dr. McElfresh's 55-year career, the first and the last person he delivered as babies joined him on stage. Alice Wood was the last baby that Dr. McElfresh helped deliver. She was three years old at the time of the ceremony. (Courtesy of Alice Darst.)

Roy Jackson stands next to his first cab on March 3, 1946. The leading taxicab service in the area, Jackson's Cab Service, lasted nearly 30 years, ending in the early 1970s. Jackson was known as an affable and reliable driver, and his cabs were well known throughout Point Pleasant, Gallipolis, and Henderson. (Courtesy of Barbara Spurlock.)

The Spencer Hotel was sold to the Lowe family in 1929 after the stock market crash of that year. Renamed the Lowe Hotel, it remained the heart of Point Pleasant's business district. This postcard of the Lowe in the middle of the 20th century boasts of its many amenities, including "steam heat" and "comfortably furnished and attractively decorated rooms." (Courtesy of Mike Brown.)

Officer Walter Rice writes a parking ticket on Sixth Street. During the school year, Rice acted as crossing guard for the Central schoolchildren. Behind him is the entrance ramp to the Silver Bridge. (Courtesy of Carolin Harris.)

LIVE MODERN ...

ENJOY A MODERN MOVIE

VISIT THE

STATE

THEATRE

POINT PLEASANT

The State Theater was the longest-lasting movie theater in Point Pleasant, beginning in the 1940s and continuing through the 1980s. Located a block from the Silver Bridge, it was easily accessible for people on both sides of the river, its marquee visible to bridge traffic throughout the night. (Courtesy of Karen Fridley.)

The Point Pleasant jailhouse stood across the street from the Mason County Court House. It was torn down when the new courthouse was built in 1958. Prisoners in the jail would throw money to schoolchildren as they passed, asking them to buy cigarettes and other items from nearby stores. Wesley Spence stops for a cigarette in front of the jailhouse in 1958 (below). An unidentified deputy (left) and Andy Galford (right), a member of the state police, relax on the jailhouse's porch in 1957 (left). (Courtesy of Carolin Harris.)

The Central School expanded through the 20th century, growing from a quaint, two-story school building to an intimate campus complex. An unidentified boy trudges across the schoolyard (right). The slide behind him was built for emergency purposes in the 1950s as a fire escape. Three children pose in front of the corollary school building (below). Originally used as the high school building, the structure had since been used for storage and the outflow of classrooms. The children are, from left to right, (first row) Carolin Harris and Marge Doris Gillespie; Corky Bates stands in the back row. (Courtesy of Carolin Harris.)

RE-ELECT

EUGENE "GENE" BALL

TO THE

HOUSE OF DELEGATES

★ Experienced

★ Honest

★ Capable

★ Trustworthy

Eugene "Gene" Ball was born on June 6, 1921. He began a dining establishment, working under a Bob Evans franchise in 1950. Over the next decade, he put together his own diner in Point Pleasant, originally located next to the jailhouse on Sixth Street. During the late 1960s, he ran and was elected into the House of Delegates. He served as a member of this house for three terms, from 1968 until 1972. This flyer was handed out during his political campaigns. He died during a reelection campaign on November 7, 1972. (Courtesy of Carolin Harris.)

Gene Ball's Restaurant was a popular Point Pleasant diner in the 1950s and 1960s (below). The main diner had a seating capacity of 110 people, including outdoor tables and a lunch counter. Down the road, Gene Ball's diner operated a drive-through establishment for diners on the run. The lunch counter was almost always crowded, as seen in the picture above. At the counter, from left to right are John Oshel, Sheryl Midkif, and Cora Edna Harris. The restaurant's motto was "A stranger is a friend we never met." (Courtesy of Mike Brown and Carolin Harris.)

Members of the junior high school marching band saunter down Main Street during one of Point Pleasant's many parades (below). Pictured from left to right, the children are Art Gilwicks (trumpet), Suzy Call (cymbals), Johnny Wamsley (snare drum), Eddie Kincaid Jr. (snare drum), and John McDermitt (cymbals). During a lull in the parade, Wayne Kincaid Jr. (above) practices his sousaphone to an unsuspecting crowd in front of the Lowe Hotel. (Courtesy of Eddie and Mary Sue Kincaid.)

Jackson's cab company, as a contributing member in the Point Pleasant community, participated yearly in the Fourth of July parade in downtown Point Pleasant. Covering one of the cabs in flowers, streamers, paper, and fabric, the cab strolled down the streets it knew so well, another positive member in the celebration. (Courtesy of Barbara Spurlock.)

Parades were always popular throughout Point Pleasant's history. Sometimes they were even exclusively in celebration of its history. This old-fashioned horse and buggy cajoles past Jackson Cab Service during a parade in 1959. One of the most popular parades from this time was Bargain Days, when the community dressed in old-fashioned garb and celebrated their pioneer history. (Courtesy of Eddie and Mary Sue Kincaid.)

Students gather around the football field in 1964 after a football game at Point Pleasant High School's Sanders Memorial Stadium. Like many schools around the country, the weekly, Friday night football games in the fall were a popular spot for teenagers and the community. The football stadium was named after Coach Marion M. Sanders, who arrived at the high school in 1942. (Courtesy of Karen Fridley.)

During the Christmas season in the 1960s, the teachers of Point Pleasant High School would organize a Christmas tree lot in part to celebrate the season as well as a fund-raiser for the high school. (Courtesy of Karen Fridley.)

86

The Big Black marching band, representing Point Pleasant High School, won numerous distinctions in 1961 and 1962. Among their normal activities at football games and at competitions, the Big Blacks' 80 members performed at the West Virginia State Fair, the Strawberry Festival, and the Black Walnut Festival. (Courtesy of the Ball family.)

The *Point Pleasant Register* moved into its current building after a fire destroyed its previous offices on Fifth and Main Streets. These men investigate the damage wrought by the inferno, particularly to its antique printing press. The damage to the building was a fortuitous impetus for the *Register* to find a new home. (Courtesy of the *Point Pleasant Register*.)

Harley Warrick (above) was a famous barn painter, known for his depictions of rural gothic America. Among many other barn painters in the 1940s, 1950s, and 1960s, he traveled throughout rural America painting large advertisements for Mail Pouch tobacco. One of his barn paintings is located on a farm outside of Point Pleasant (below), and has remained there, with only periodic touch-ups since the early 1960s. His barns are now considered state treasures. (Courtesy of Karen Fridley.)

Cameron Charles Lewis (right) was president of Citizen's National Bank (below) from 1929 until 1963. He began his tenure as president one month before the stock market crash. Formerly Merchants National Bank of Point Pleasant, Lewis guided the bank through the tough economic turmoil following the market crash. A descendant of Col. Charles Lewis, who died at the Battle of Point Pleasant, and Andrew Lewis, who led the Virginia militia at this battle, he was among the group that organized the 1909 commemoration of that battle. (Courtesy of Rod Brand.)

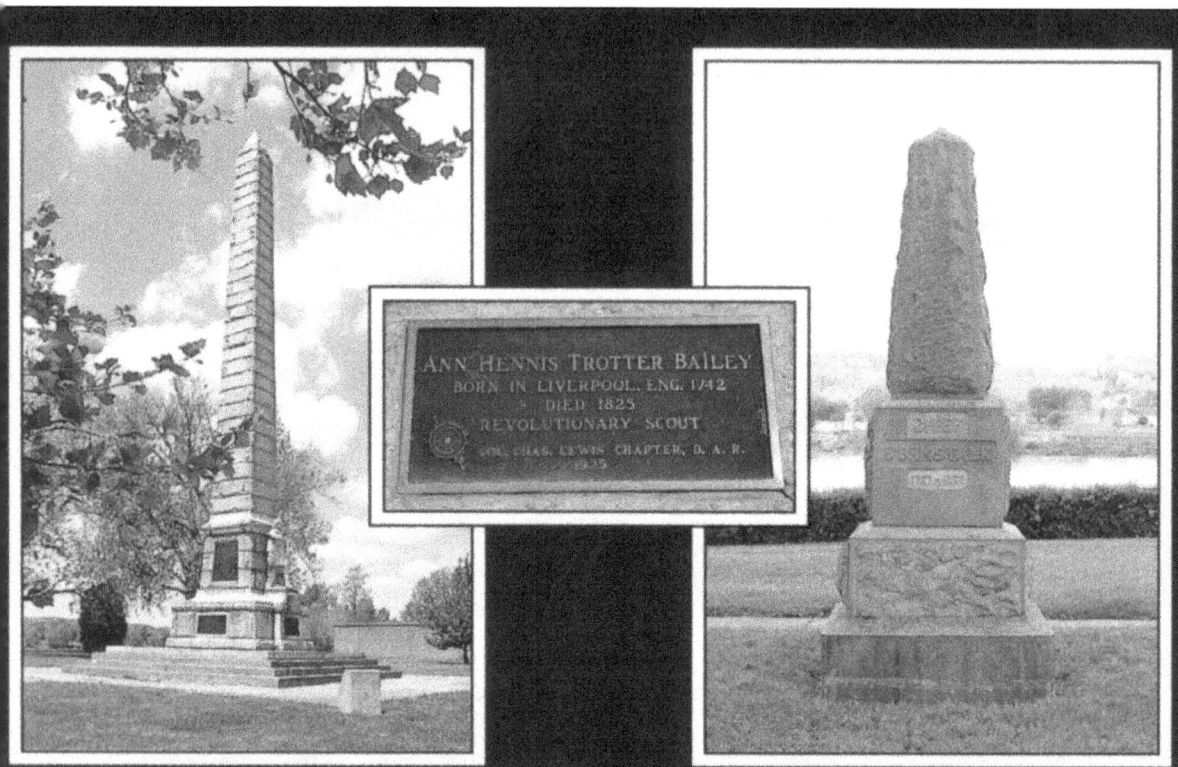

When Chief Cornstalk's grave (right) was relocated to Tu-Endie-Wei in 1958, his remains joined those of the other important historical personages of Point Pleasant. The giant obelisk (left) commemorates the soldiers who died at the Battle of Point Pleasant, all of whom are buried there. Cornstalk was originally murdered at Fort Randolph, when it stood at Tu-Endie-Wei in 1777. The middle grave belongs to "Mad" Anne Bailey, a pioneer woman who served as scout and messenger to the forts and outposts in the area. She also served as the first postal worker in Point Pleasant, delivering mail for 25¢ a letter. (Courtesy of Mike Brown.)

The Mason County Court House was torn down and rebuilt in 1958. Constructed for $750,000, it replaced the previous courthouse, which stood for nearly a century in its previous incarnation. In 1963, the courthouse expanded, converting a former American Legion hall into offices. In 1976, a man detonated a suitcase filled with dynamite in the basement of the courthouse, destroying the cell block area. That annex was reconstructed within the next year. (Courtesy of Mike Brown.)

In 1966, the old Phoenix Hotel building was torn down. In it place would be built G. C. Murphy's, a local department store, newest expansion. The Phoenix Hotel was built in 1874 and operated as a hotel until the 1930s. The hotel's most memorable components were its lunchroom and poolroom, owned and operated by William Burdette. (Courtesy of the Point Pleasant Post Office.)

The Ashland oil station stood on the corner of Viand and Second Street in close proximity to the Shadle Bridge. In this picture, a much needed sidewalk is being poured, allowing pedestrian traffic around this section of downtown to flow with smoother efficiency. (Courtesy of the Point Pleasant Post Office.)

Five

THE SILVER BRIDGE DISASTER

The day the Silver Bridge collapsed under its own pressure into the Ohio River taking 46 innocent souls is a day that will be stitched into the city's memory for many years to come. After 40 years of neglect and disservice, the Silver Bridge buckled, shook, and fell into the river. Point Pleasant and the nearby communities were struck to its core.

The bridge fell as the result of an eyebar, a part of its suspension system, fracturing from the intense pressure and overwhelming strain on its steel body. Like a strand of dominoes, after one eyebar snapped, the rest followed. Within a minute, the entire bridge sunk in the river. Rescue efforts began immediately and did not stop for weeks.

The Silver Bridge collapsed because it could not handle the pressure of its own modernity. Built in lighter times, when Model Ts crossed its span, it could not deal with the ever-increasing chassis of automobiles in the 1960s. The average car was more than double the size of the car in 1928, and the result of that shortsightedness was the bridge disaster. After the bridge fell, a complete overhaul of the bridge inspection system took place, hoping to avoid another disaster like the one in Point Pleasant. While the Silver Bridge was unique in America, its story might not have been, and this disaster most likely prevented countless others.

The location of a bridge across the Ohio River between Point Pleasant, West Virginia, and Gallipolis, Ohio, was approved by the Army Corps of Engineers and the Assistant Secretary of War in March 1927. The construction of the Silver Bridge began on May 1, 1927, while the entire project was completed on May 19, 1928. It was originally constructed for Gallia County Ohio River Bridge Company. The bridge was a unique brand of suspension bridge, the entire structure supported by eyebars strewn along the long cables between the towers. (Courtesy of the Point Pleasant River Museum.)

The Silver Bridge was dedicated on May 30, 1928. The first people to cross the bridge were Robert Heslop (on horse, left) and James D. Robinson (on horse, right). Together they rode across the bridge on the horse, Old May. An act of Congress in 1926 authorized the building of this bridge. (Courtesy of the Point Pleasant River Museum.)

The Silver Bridge towers were unique and innovative designs for bridges of the time. Over 130 feet high, these towers were known as "rockers." They had the ability to sway with the variations in chain lengths and shifting loads due to temperature fluxes. Dowel rods prevented the towers from shifting horizontally with these variations. These towers were not fixed to their bases, either, allowing greater ability for movement. These pictures, depicting the northern (below) and southern (left) views from one of the towers, were taken during the towers' construction. (Courtesy of the Point Pleasant River Museum.)

The total length of the Silver Bridge was 2,235 feet, including both approach ramps. The bridge had a roadway width of 22 feet, with a 6-foot-wide sidewalk along one edge. Over 6,000 vehicles crossed it daily before it fell in 1967. (Courtesy of Mike Brown.)

SILVER BRIDGE, GALLIPOLIS, OHIO   H-718

On the Ohio side of the Silver Bridge was a toll house. The bridge operated as a toll bridge from 1928 until 1951. The State of West Virginia bought the bridge in 1941 for a price of $1,040,000. It closed the tollbooth and opened the bridge up as a free, public bridge a decade later. (Courtesy of Mike Brown.)

A postcard from the 1940s depicts the Silver Bridge from the Ohio side of the river. While officially named the Ohio–West Virginia Bridge, it was nicknamed the "Silver Bridge" because of its gleaming aluminum paint, the first bridge in the area to be painted as such. (Courtesy of Mike Brown.)

An aerial photograph of the Ohio River shows the full spectrum of the damage to the bridge. Where the Silver Bridge once stood as a connection between two communities, only the tower bases remained, protruding from the water like jagged teeth. (Courtesy of Barbara Spurlock.)

The approach ramp on the Ohio shore was effectively destroyed with the bridge collapse. The West Virginia approach was the only part of the bridge that remained intact. The state of Ohio enacted mandatory bridge inspections immediately following the Silver Bridge collapse. The state of West Virginia did not order any bridge inspections until a nationwide bridge inspection act was created by Congress. (Courtesy of Barbara Spurlock.)

An engineer stands on the remains of the entrance ramp on the Ohio bank. Traffic between the two states was rerouted to the nearest bridge, 14 miles upriver around Mason, West Virginia, and Pomeroy, Ohio. Citizens of both states used the Silver Bridge as part of the highway connecting Charleston, West Virginia, and Chillicothe, Ohio. (Courtesy of the Point Pleasant River Museum.)

People watch from the shore as the recovery efforts are underway. While the entire community was stunned from this tragic event, they did not stay idle. The Red Cross had 150 volunteers, many of them local, working around the clock, preparing meals for boat operators, helping in the hospital, and clearing debris and rubble, all in the an effort to heal the wounds of this disaster. (Courtesy of the Point Pleasant River Museum.)

Near one of the tower bases, a diver prepares for a plunge into the river's depths, searching for victims. The murky water, sharp metal debris, and pervasive aquatic life made the search difficult. Visibility and temperatures were extremely low. Only two bodies were never recovered. (Courtesy of Barbara Spurlock.)

Boats dredge the river along the Ohio bank. Many of the locks and dams upriver from this position were closed in order to reduce the current and allow for easier traversing for recovery crews. River traffic was stalled for days following the bridge collapse, the only boats allowed along this section of the river were those being utilized for the salvaging. (Courtesy of Barbara Spurlock.)

On the West Virginia shore, a towboat dredges the riverbank. M. F. Epling was one of many local companies that volunteered their services in the rescue effort. Based out of Gallipolis, this company was especially effective in removing sand and gravel, as well as other debris. (Courtesy of Barbara Spurlock.)

Once rescue boats and derricks arrived at the scene, many of them operated by the Army Corps of Engineers, it took seven hours before the first car could be removed from water. The wreckage from the bridge spans was a gnarled mess, a metal morass that made rescue nearly impossible. (Courtesy of Barbara Spurlock.)

Astonished onlookers gaze at a car being lifted near the bridge's beams. Reports from eyewitnesses claimed that the bridge folded "like a stack of cards," in a very quick fashion. The investigative committee estimated that the bridge collapsed within 60 seconds, from the western side to the eastern side. (Courtesy of Barbara Spurlock.)

An amphibious vehicle enters the water during the recovery effort, joining the fleet of barges, towboats, and other watercraft hoping to retrieve the victims' bodies and their vehicles from the river. (Courtesy of the Point Pleasant River Museum.)

When the towboats and other watercraft removed the cars from the river, they were placed together in a nearby lot. Thirty-one of 37 vehicles on the bridge fell into the water when the bridge collapsed, while the other six either fell to the shore or managed to stay on the entrance ramp. (Courtesy of the Point Pleasant River Museum.)

A ground-level view of a fallen truck portrays the devastation achieved by the bridge collapse. To the right and above the truck rests two of the fallen eyebars that held the bridge in place and made it such a unique style of suspension bridge. (Courtesy of Barbara Spurlock.)

An engineer on the Ohio bank poses in front of the ruins. The unidentified man stands near the point where the bridge's entrance ramp stood. In the background, a crane lifts some of the bridge's remains out from the water and onto the shore. (Courtesy of Barbara Spurlock.)

This car, driven by a man from Gallipolis, was on the approach ramp when the Silver Bridge collapsed. The car stayed on top of a concrete block of the ramp, riding the block as it fell from the ramp structure and landed on the ground. Luckily, none of the passengers in the car were injured, nor was the car badly damaged. (Courtesy of Barbara Spurlock.)

Much of the bridge debris dwarfed the people who attempted to remove it from the river. Despite its plunge into the river, large portions of metal and concrete remained whole. The recovery was a massive project requiring intense coordination between teams of boats and individuals. The man in charge of the recovery was Andy Wilson, a local man from Civil Defense. (Courtesy of Barbara Spurlock.)

On the Ohio shore, engineers and other members of the recovery team assess the bridge damage. The Army Corps of Engineers and the National Guard were instrumental to the recovery effort, leading much of the way through the chaos ensuing after the tragedy occurred. (Courtesy of Barbara Spurlock.)

Two cranes were the first to arrive to the scene, located just upriver from the bridge. Along with the Coast Guard, which had a post near Point Pleasant, they appeared at the bridge site within minutes of the collapse, a heroic reaction to the calls for help. (Courtesy of Barbara Spurlock.)

This McLean truck driver was injured when the bridge fell, his back broken. His passenger, however, did not survive the fall. This truck was the closest vehicle to the Ohio shore to not escape the bridge's collapse. Nine cars were ahead of this truck and all drove off in relative safety. The McLean truck did not make it off the bridge. The investigative committee, inspecting the cause of the bridge's collapse, also determined the layout of every car on the bridge during its fall. Going from west to east in numerical order, the McLean truck was number 10, while the nine cars ahead of it were numbers 1 through 9. Out of 38 vehicles on the bridge, all the cars from 10 through 37 fell with the bridge, with the majority of their passengers dying. (Courtesy of Barbara Spurlock.)

Heavy cranes, such as the one seen behind the ramp, were key assets in the Silver Bridge recovery efforts. The Army Corps of Engineers utilized their largest derrick crane during this mission. The crane was capable of lifting objects weighing over 100 tons. (Courtesy of Barbara Spurlock.)

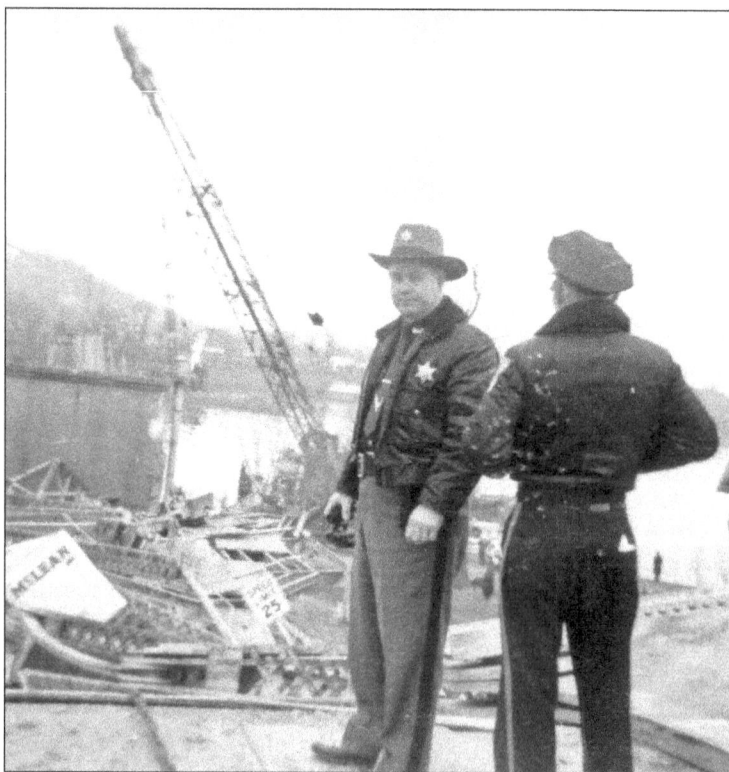

Even in the midst of a local tragedy, citizens of Point Pleasant joined the National Guard and the Corps of Engineers in the recovery effort. Millard Halstead (left), chief deputy sheriff of Mason County, and another city police officer observe the destruction. As local law agents, their primary duty was to keep the peace on land, attempting to calm the nerves of a shaken community. (Courtesy of Barbara Spurlock.)

Six

AFTER THE FALL

There were two major factors that led to the negative growth of Point Pleasant: the closing of the Marietta Manufacturing Corporation and the collapse of the Silver Bridge. Both events occurred in 1967, and while they are not directly related, these incidents were indicative of a growing national trend that led to the steady demise of a once-thriving town. This trend is the country's burgeoning highway system and the shift from river traffic to interstate traffic.

When the Silver Bridge fell, the local highway was rerouted to completely bypass Point Pleasant. Where the Silver Bridge led people directly to the heart of Point Pleasant, the Silver Memorial Bridge, built shortly after the bridge collapse and downriver from the original, enabled motorists an oblique route around the city instead of through it. Main Street businesses were not able to deal with the loss of traffic.

The Marietta Manufacturing plant closed in 1967, forcing numerous men and women in the area into unemployment. The plant's closing marked a new era for transportation, as the riverboats, barges, and other water vessels were not the dominant form of mass transit. After 50 years in town, Point Pleasant had trouble adapting to life without its major source of industry.

This time, while a major struggle economically, was also a very creative time in Point Pleasant. In 1974, the town celebrated the bicentennial of the Battle of Point Pleasant, marking a huge milestone for Point Pleasant's history. This celebration began a trend of the town remembering its past and renewing it. Fort Randolph was rebuilt for the bicentennial, erected again after 180 years. The West Virginia State Farm Museum, utilizing some of the former TNT area, was built, a commemoration of the enduring history of Point Pleasant's agriculture, which has never relented since the town's formation. Point Pleasant spent the years following a major tragedy to reflect on its past in the hopes of a brighter future.

An aerial view of Point Pleasant in the 1970s shows much of the river around the city. During its history, Point Pleasant experienced intense moments of contamination, as the dark black of the Ohio River shows. Because the city is downriver from multiple power plants, water and soil conservation became top priorities for the city in the latter half of the 20th century and well into the 21st century. (Courtesy of the USDA.)

After World War II, the TNT area was decommissioned as an ordnance area. The buildings remained, but all of the land was left to nature's devices. Within 50 years, it became a wildlife management area. Open to the public, the stark beauty of its pools and forests is in sharp contrast to the decaying buildings, concrete bunkers, and empty warehouses that continue to litter the area. (Courtesy of West Virginia State Farm Museum.)

The Mason County Library was built in the 1970s on the same lot as the old Central School. While the school stood for nearly 80 years, the school's old-fashioned pull bell and iron fence remain as a part of the library, remembrances of the historical structure before it. (Courtesy of the West Virginia State Farm Museum.)

An early form of e-mail, E-COM (Electronic Computer Originated Mail) messages were dispatches sent electronically through telephone lines between post offices. For a fee, a person's message was transmitted, printed, and delivered to its recipient. This is the first E-COM message used in West Virginia. The most notable aspect of this message is the passage welcoming West Virginia to the Computer Age in 1982. (Courtesy of the Point Pleasant Post Office.)

```
Credit Bureau of
Point Pleasant, Inc.
P. O. Box 412
Pt Pleasant WV  25550-0412
12-MAY-82 1738 1004 10003
12-MAY-82 1924 M926 PIT NA

Q. A. (Al) Biggs,
Postmaster
Pt Pleasant WV  25550-9998

FIRST E-COM MESSAGE IN WEST VIRGINIA
PRESS RELEASE

May 12, 1982

Another first for historical Point Pleasant, West Virginia,
the site of the first battle of the American Revolution on
October 10, 1774.

Wednesday, May 12, 1982 marks the first transmission of the
U. S. Postal Service's Electronic Computer Originated Mail
(E-COM) in the great state of West Virginia.

          "WELCOME TO THE COMPUTER AGE"

          Robert (Bob) Cochran
          President, Credit Bureau
          Point Pleasant, WV  25550-0412

          Q. A. (Al) Biggs
          Postmaster
          Point Pleasant, WV  25550-9998

          Software Laboratories, Inc.
          6924 Riverside Drive
          Dublin, OH  43017
```

Gene Ball's Restaurant burned to the ground in 1970, ending its 20-year reign as a favorite restaurant among local Point Pleasantians. Even though Ball was already an elected official in the House of Delegates by the time the diner burned, he always kept his roots close to him, keeping the diner's motto "A Stranger is a friend I've never met" in his public life. (Courtesy of the Ball family.)

Mary Berkeley (left) and Carolin Harris (right) stand in front of Harris' Steakhouse in 1970. The sign in the restaurant's window welcomes Maj. Hayden Lockhart home from service in Vietnam. Lockhart had been a prisoner of war during his tour of duty and had recently been released. (Courtesy of Carolin Harris.)

The dedication of Fort Randolph (right) took place on the bicentennial of the Battle of Point Pleasant, October 10, 1974. Speaking at the podium is Gov. Arch Moore, as Jack Burdette (seated left) and Rev. Tally Hanna (seated right) listen to his speech. The fort (below) is a reproduction, exact in scale, of the original fort that stood for several years at Tu-Endie-Wei before it was burned down in the late 18th century. It was at this fort that Chief Cornstalk was murdered in 1777. The reproduction now resides in Krodel Park, and an annual reenactment of the death of Cornstalk and the ensuing siege is produced every spring. (Courtesy of Rod Brand and the West Virginia State Farm Museum.)

The employees of the Citizen's National Bank pose for a group photograph. Dressed in pioneer garb, they are celebrating the bicentennial of the Battle of Point Pleasant, which occurred in October 1774. The bicentennial was an enormous affair for Point Pleasant, not only as a celebration of the city's history, but also as a continuation of the commemorative tradition and pioneer spirit of the town. (Courtesy of Rod Brand.)

Lona Fridley Jones was a teacher in Mason County for 55 years, beginning her career in the one-room schoolhouses in the rural parts of the county. She is the author of a book on West Virginia history, called *The Gateway to the Golden Horseshoe*. In this picture, a local civic group awards her for her contribution to the state's education. She was the first educator in Mason County to receive an Honorary Golden Horseshoe Pin. (Courtesy of Karen Fridley.)

This building, at the corner of Sixth and Main Streets, began as the offices of the Doctors Andrew and Hugh Barbee, who operated out of the second floor. The first floor housed the post office from 1901 until 1913, and the top floor was the Masonic Hall. By the end of the 20th century, the once-prestigious building stayed empty or housed liquor stores. (Courtesy of Rod Brand.)

Christ Episcopal Church was organized on July 20, 1867. Its first church was built in 1873 for a price of $6,000. The 1913 flood destroyed much of the inside of the church. A new one was built in 1923 but was heavily burned in 1963. After the renovation, the church remains one of the most ornate in Point Pleasant, as seen in this picture from the 1970s. (Courtesy of Rod Brand.)

On March 2, 1976, Bruce Sisk, armed with a shotgun and a suitcase full of dynamite, forced his way into the jail cell of the courthouse where his wife was detained for the suspected murder of his infant child. While Sheriff Elvin "Pete" Wedge and other deputies negotiated with Sisk outside of the basement jail cell, Sisk detonated the dynamite, killing himself and four other people and injuring 11 others. The courthouse explosion rocked Point Pleasant, which was still reeling from the Silver Bridge disaster a decade earlier. The entire first floor of the jailhouse collapsed into the basement level (above), while the devastation of the dynamite eroded the infrastructure of the entire jail cell block (left). (Courtesy of the Mason County Library.)

Sheriff Elvin "Pete" Wedge (above) was killed in the courthouse explosion on March 2, 1976. He died courageously as he negotiated with the bomber, who detonated the bomb before Sheriff Wedge could clear the building of hostages. He had already served for three years as sheriff of Mason County and was working on a reelection campaign. At the funeral for the three fallen police officers (below), over 100 state troopers, police officers, and elected officials from around West Virginia paid their respects for Sheriff Wedge and the other brave men. (Courtesy of the Mason County Library.)

Mario Libertore (middle) poses with Howard Schultz (right) and Walden Roush (left). Both Roush and Schultz were prominent members of the Mason County Board of Education and instrumental in the formation of the West Virginia State Farm Museum. Mario Libertore was a noted banker in Point Pleasant and a generous donator to the community. (Courtesy of Rod Brand.)

The board of directors of Citizens National Bank takes a group photograph. These men, like their predecessors during the days of the Merchants National Bank, were important contributors to the Point Pleasant community, particularly in the business domain and the foundation of public projects. The men are, from left to right, (first row) James H. Lewis, William Rardin, and C. C. Lewis Jr.; (second row) Charles Lanham and Mario Libertore; (third row) Charles Hyer, R. G. Green, and E. Bartow Jones. (Courtesy of Rod Brand.)

John Greene, from Milton, West Virginia, donated the first buildings for the West Virginia State Farm Museum in 1976. The Greene building, a vast warehouse of farming antiquities and West Virginia artifacts, was the original building of the Farm Museum. Greene also donated the museum's blacksmith shop and country kitchen. (Courtesy of the West Virginia State Farm Museum.)

The West Virginia State Farm Museum (then the Mason County Farm Museum) is recognized by the West Virginia Agricultural Hall of Fame Foundation in 1980. The men are, from left to right, Gus Douglass, a native Mason Countian and the commissioner of agriculture; John Greene; an unidentified man; and Walden Roush. (Courtesy of the West Virginia State Farm Museum.)

This horse, named General, is the third-largest horse in recorded history. He stood 19 and a half hands high and weighed 2,850 pounds. Born in 1971, he was the largest horse in the world while he was alive. He was a registered Belgian Gelding and was named grand champion at Toronto's Royal Winter Fair. He lived his final years at the West Virginia State Farm Museum. He died in 1982, and his body has been preserved. He now lives forever in a specially made barn at the West Virginia State Farm Museum. (Courtesy of Karen Fridley.)

Walden Roush poses with his wife, Louise, at the West Virginia State Farm Museum. Walden was superintendent of schools in Mason County for 11 years and was on the board of education for many more. A lifelong teacher, upon retirement he decided to continue educating the public through charitable works. He was the first executive director of the local chamber of commerce and bought part of the old TNT area to be used by industrial companies. He also organized the West Virginia State Farm Museum in this area, starting in 1976, and served as its director for over 15 years. (Courtesy of the West Virginia State Farm Museum.)

In the decades following the Silver Bridge disaster, the once-thriving business district of Point Pleasant broke down, no longer sufficiently maintained by a steady flow of traffic running through town from the Silver Bridge. Many of these buildings (above), during the 1980s, are located at the bottom of where the Silver Bridge would have been. Mostly abandoned at this point in time, the shopping crowds and interested parties were no longer readily available. Main Street fared a similar fate (below). The State Theater, once a shining beacon even in the nighttime, had fallen into disrepair and failure. (Courtesy of Rod Brand.)

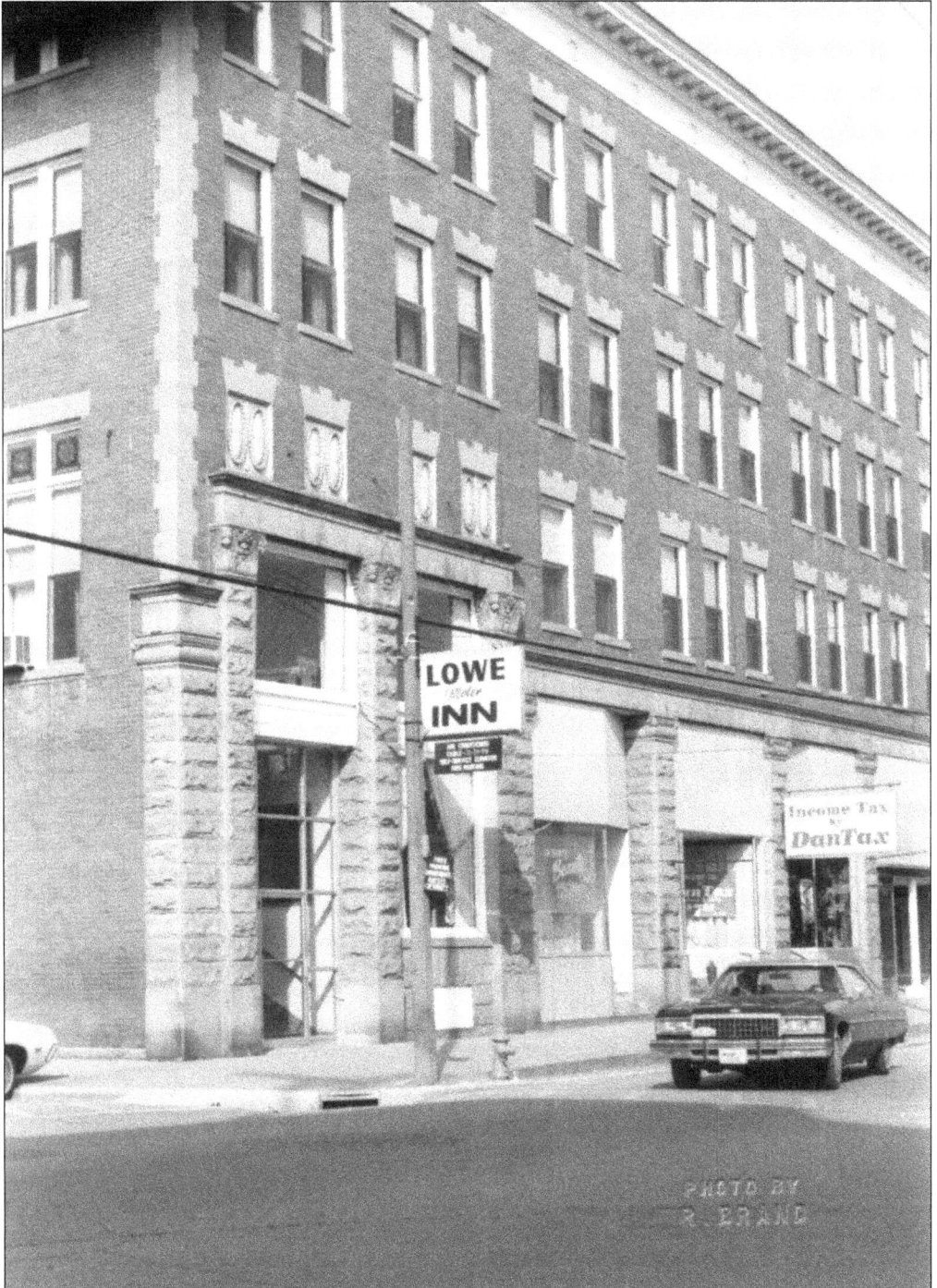

Even after eight decades, the Lowe Hotel still managed to stand firm. In its walls beat the heart of the city. During the 1980s, a decidedly lean year for the hotel and other businesses in the area, the Lowe managed to stay open, surviving when other businesses died out. The Lowe continued its traditional of exceptional quality and decorative fancy, keeping alive the decades of grandeur that linger in the streets, waiting to emerge again. (Courtesy of Rod Brand.)

By 1940, Hooff's Opera House held its final performance in its performance hall. The glamour and elegance of the Opera House could not compete with the movie theaters springing up throughout town, as public interest switched from live theater to the glitz of Hollywood. Within the next two decades, the elevated stage, with its beautifully ornate backdrops, the two-tiered dressing rooms, the upper level seating known as "peanut heaven," and every other distinguishing feature of this grand ole Opera House was steadily converted into offices and apartments. Today the imposing outer frame stands out among the empty buildings on Main Street. The only trace of the Hooff's former glory is the dilapidated livery stables behind the building. (Courtesy of Rod Brand.)

After half a century of wear and tear, the Shadle Bridge began a continual decline. The thin roadway leading through the bridge could not keep up with the traffic demands of modern vehicles (above). By the middle of the 1990s, a public movement began, demanding the erection of a new bridge to replace the slowly decaying Shadle Bridge. By 1996, the Bartow Jones Bridge was under construction (below), a modern bridge for a freshly modern town. Named after a noted member of the Point Pleasant community, the Bartow Jones Bridge already dwarfed the decrepit Shadle Bridge by the time it was only halfway constructed. (Courtesy of the City of Point Pleasant.)

The Shadle Bridge was demolished on December 16, 1998, thirty-one years and one day after the last bridge demolition in Point Pleasant history. In the cold morning, workers cleared the area of any pedestrians, removed people from homes near the bridge, and took every safety precaution. Crowds milled as close to the spectacle as they could, far enough away to avoid any injury, but close enough to see the bridge buckle under the explosions. When the charges were detonated, the bridge imploded, caving into the Kanawha River (above). The only peripheral damage was to an apartment building's window. When the dust settled and the crowds cheered, the resulting image was one not uncommon to Point Pleasant (below). The major difference, however, was that this bridge was meant to collapse. (Courtesy of the City of Point Pleasant.)

BIBLIOGRAPHY

Brown, Lisle G. *The History of the Marietta Manufacturing Company*. Huntington, WV: Marshall University Press, 2006.

The Citizen. Point Pleasant, WV: 1937.

Graham, Philip. *Showboats*. Austin, TX: University of Texas Press, 1951.

Kraina, Jane M. *The Fall of the Silver Bridge*. Charleston, WV: West Virginia Division of Culture and History, 1995.

LeRose, Chris. *The Collapse of the Silver Bridge*. Charleston, WV: West Virginia Historical Society, 2001.

Mason County History Book Commission, *History of Mason County, West Virginia, 1987*. Waynesville, NC: Walsworth Publishing Company, 1987.

Mason Republican. Point Pleasant, WV: 1907, 1913.

Point Pleasant Register. Point Pleasant, WV: 1913, 1937, 1967.

Sutphin, Gerald. *Sternwheelers on the Great Kanawha River*. Charleston, WV: Pictorial Histories Publishing, 1991.

State Gazette. Point Pleasant, WV: 1937.

The Herald-Dispatch. Huntington, WV. 1967, 1968.

Way, Frederick, Jr. *Way's Packet Directory, 1848–1983*. Athens, OH: Ohio University Press, 1983.

———. *Way's Steam Towboat Directory*. Athens, OH: Ohio University Press, 1990.

Visit us at
arcadiapublishing.com

. . . .